HSC

Dear Parent:

Congratulations! Your child is taking the first steps on an exciting journey. The destination? Independent reading!

STEP INTO READING® will help your child get there. The program offers books at five levels that accompany children from their first attempts at reading to reading success. Each step includes fun stories, fiction and nonfiction, and colorful art. There are also Step into Reading Sticker Books, Step into Reading Math Readers, and Step into Reading Phonics Readers—a complete literacy program with something to interest every child.

Learning to Read, Step by Step!

Ready to Read   Preschool–Kindergarten
• big type and easy words • rhyme and rhythm • picture clues
For children who know the alphabet and are eager to begin reading.

Reading with Help   Preschool–Grade 1
• basic vocabulary • short sentences • simple stories
For children who recognize familiar words and sound out new words with help.

Reading on Your Own   Grades 1–3
• engaging characters • easy-to-follow plots • popular topics
For children who are ready to read on their own.

Reading Paragraphs   Grades 2–3
• challenging vocabulary • short paragraphs • exciting stories
For newly independent readers who read simple sentences with confidence.

Ready for Chapters   Grades 2–4
• chapters • longer paragraphs • full-color art
For children who want to take the plunge into chapter books but still like colorful pictures.

STEP INTO READING® is designed to give every child a successful reading experience. The grade levels are only guides. Children can progress through the steps at their own speed, developing confidence in their reading, no matter what their grade.

Remember, a lifetime love of reading starts with a single step!

To Julie Strickland,
who does good things for kids
—D.L.H.

In memory of Grandpa Wohnoutka
—M.W.

Text copyright © 2001 by David L. Harrison.
Illustrations copyright © 2001 by Mike Wohnoutka.
All rights reserved under International and Pan-American Copyright Conventions.
Published in the United States by Random House Children's Books, a division of
Random House, Inc., New York, and simultaneously in Canada by Random House
of Canada Limited, Toronto.

www.stepintoreading.com

Educators and librarians, for a variety of teaching tools, visit us at
www.randomhouse.com/teachers

Library of Congress Cataloging-in-Publication Data
Harrison, David Lee, 1937– .
Johnny Appleseed : my story / by David L. Harrison ; illustrated by Mike Wohnoutka.
    p.   cm. — (Step into reading. A step 3 book)
SUMMARY: An introduction to the life of the man who traveled west planting apple seeds
to make the country a better place to live, as told from his perspective.
ISBN 0-375-81247-4 (trade) — ISBN 0-375-91247-9 (lib. bdg.)
1. Appleseed, Johnny, 1774–1845—Juvenile literature. 2. Apple growers—United States—
Biography—Juvenile literature. 3. Frontier and pioneer life—Middle West—Juvenile literature.
[1. Appleseed, Johnny, 1774–1845. 2. Apple growers. 3. Frontier and pioneer life.]
I. Wohnoutka, Mike, ill. II. Title. III. Series: Step into reading. Step 3 book.
SB63 .C46 H37 2003 634' .11'092—dc21 2002013224

Printed in the United States of America 15 14 13 12 11 10 9 8 7 6

STEP INTO READING, RANDOM HOUSE, and the Random House colophon are registered
trademarks of Random House, Inc.

Johnny Appleseed
My Story

by David L. Harrison
illustrated by Mike Wohnoutka

Random House 🏠 New York

"Someone is coming!"
Beth yelled.
It was a lean, wiry man
with pep in his step.
"Mama! Papa!" cried Will.
"It's Johnny!"
It was Johnny Appleseed!

Papa stopped chopping wood.

"Johnny Appleseed is

always welcome!" Papa said.

"He always has

a good tale to tell."

Johnny smiled

and waved hello.

Mama invited him

to stay for supper.

Beth and Will were so excited.

They jumped up and down.

"Tell us a story!" they begged.

Johnny scratched his chin.

His eyes were kind.

"You children are growing

like tree sprouts!" he said.

"I *will* tell you a story.

After I help your papa

chop wood."

Johnny was good with an ax!

He chopped and chopped.

At dinner,

Johnny ate all he could.

He told Mama,

"I walked twenty miles

to get here.

Your pie was worth every step!"

He winked at Beth and Will.

"Now for a story," he said.

Beth and Will

sat on the floor.

They loved stories.

Johnny began like this.

"My real name is John Chapman.

I grew up in a big family."

"Ten kids!

We were noisy and raggedy.

Always barefoot.

And we were as hungry as

bear cubs in spring!"

"To be by myself,
I would head for the woods.
I knew the trees
and rivers for miles.
More and more,
the woods felt like home."

"After school, I worked
to help my family.
But when I was old enough,
I set out on my own.
I packed up my gun
and my hatchet.
I left Massachusetts,
walking west
on my bare feet!"

"Soon I came to a cider mill.
They were giving away
the seeds from the apples!
A poor boy never passes up
anything free!"

"I filled my pack with seeds.

I grinned as if those seeds

were gold!"

"But I lost that grin

in a storm in Pennsylvania.

I was walking

up in the mountains.

All at once, the day

turned as dark as night!

The wind began to howl."

"It was bitter cold.

Snow was soon

up to my waist!

If I did not do something,

I would die!"

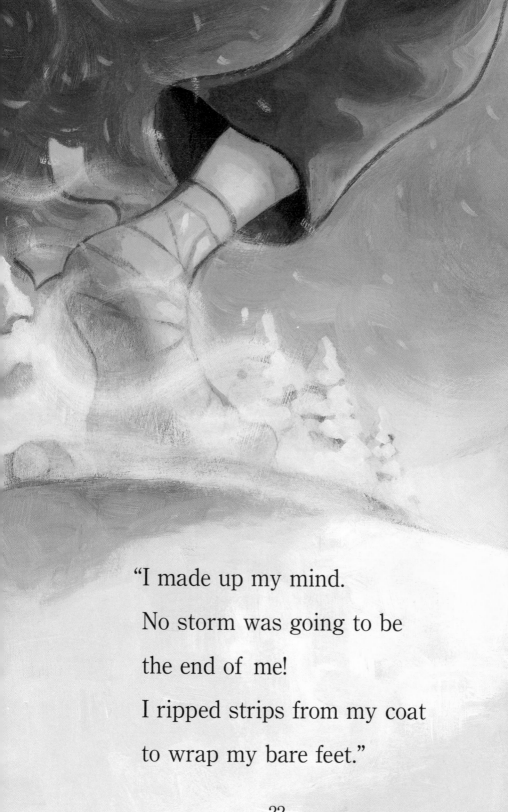

"I made up my mind.
No storm was going to be
the end of me!
I ripped strips from my coat
to wrap my bare feet."

"Then I wove snowshoes
from branches.
And I walked right out
of that storm!"

23

"Walking gave me time to think.
Folks were moving west.
What would they need
when they got there?
Apples!
I would plant an orchard!"

"I got an ax

and started clearing trees!

CHUNK! CHUNK! CHUNK!

I chopped.

I made the wood chips fly!"

"Soon my first seeds
took root and sprouted.
So I set out west
to find more land."

"I planted apple seeds
in Pennsylvania,
Ohio, and Indiana."

"I sold sprouts to folks

heading west in their wagons.

I sold sprouts to settlers

living in log cabins.

One sprout cost

six and a half cents."

"Sometimes I traded sprouts
for clothes or food.
Some folks were too poor
to trade.
I gave them sprouts for free.
I knew how it felt
to be poor."

"Most folks do not know
my real name.
They just call me
Johnny Appleseed!
I still work hard
taking care of my orchards."

"I sleep out under the stars.
And I will wear
any old clothes or hat
to keep warm."

Johnny held up his bare feet.
"But I still do not like
to wear shoes," he said.
"Unless it is winter,
I do not need them.
My feet are tough!"

"Folks say your feet are
as tough as elephant hide,"
said Beth.
"So tough that a rattlesnake
cannot bite through!"
said Will.

Johnny laughed. "There are more stories about me than fleas on a dog."

"Folks say that I can
leap over icy rivers!
Or melt ice with my
bare feet!"

"Folks say I once met
a band of men
who wanted to fight me.
I talked them into
a chopping contest instead."

"Of course, I won.
And I tricked those rascals
into helping me clear land
for a new orchard!"

"Then there are bear stories.
People say bears trust
old Johnny Appleseed.
Mama bears do not mind
if I wrestle their cubs!"

"Others say I sleep with bears
to keep warm on winter nights!
Ugh! Have you ever smelled
a bear's breath?"

"But one thing is for sure.
I know a lot of Indians!
Many are my friends.
They have taught me
their languages.
And how to hunt for food.
And how to make canoes
out of hollow logs."

Will yawned.

Beth was half asleep.

Johnny stood up.

"Time for you two
to go to bed," he said.

"And time for me
to keep walking.

There is always more
planting to be done."

Beth and Will hugged Johnny.

"Next time you visit,

you will have more stories

to tell us!" Will said.

"And more wood to chop,"

said Johnny.

"And more of Mama's pie

to eat!" Beth giggled.

Papa smiled at Johnny.

"You look like a happy man,"
Papa said.

Johnny smiled, too.

"I *am* a happy man," he said.

"I have spent my life
raising apple tree sprouts."

"Now all across the land,
folks are enjoying apples
from my trees.
And that makes me happy!"
Then Johnny Appleseed
waved good-bye.